MACKEREL SHARKS

To Mom, for teaching me that your art can make a difference

Copyright © 2017 by Lily Williams
Published by Roaring Brook Press
Roaring Brook Press is a division of Holtzbrinck Publishing Holdings Limited Partnership
120 Broadway, New York, NY 10271

mackids.com

Library of Congress Cataloging-in-Publication Data

Names: Williams, Lily.
Title: If sharks disappeared / Lily Williams.
Description: First edition. | New York : Roaring Brook Press, 2017. | Includes bibliographical references.
Identifiers: LCCN 2016035661 | ISBN 9781626724136 (hardback)
Subjects: LCSH: Sharks—Juvenile literature. | Marine animals—Juvenile literature. | Endangered species— Juvenile
    literature. | BISAC: JUVENILE NONFICTION / Animals / Marine Life. | JUVENILE NONFICTION / Animals
    / Endangered. | JUVENILE NONFICTION / Science & Nature / Earth Sciences / General.
Classification: LCC QL638.9 .W54 2017 | DDC 597.3—dc23
LC record available at https://lccn.loc.gov/2016035661

Our books may be purchased in bulk for promotional, educational, or business use. Please contact your local
bookseller or the Macmillan Corporate and Premium Sales Department at (800) 221-7945 ext. 5442 or by e-mail at
MacmillanSpecialMarkets@macmillan.com.

First edition, 2017
Book design by Elizabeth H. Clark
Printed in China by Toppan Leefung Printing Ltd., Dongguan City, Guangdong Province

9 10 8

IF SHARKS DISAPPEARED

Lily Williams

ROARING BROOK PRESS
NEW YORK

THIS IS A HEALTHY OCEAN. It's a balanced
environment where many different animals
and plants thrive. The ocean is home to a lot
of creatures—
          big,
            small,
              slimy,
                cute, and . . .

SCARY.

Sharks have helped keep our oceans balanced for about 450 million years. Over that time, they evolved into the more than 400 different species that exist today.

TALL TREES MADE FORESTS

FIRST MODERN MAMMALS

FIRST GRASSLANDS

LOTS OF DIFFERENT DINOS

Mass extinction

60-65 MILLION YEARS AGO

TODAY!

HUMANS APPEARED 200,000 YEARS AGO

MODERN SHARKS

Sharks are apex predators, which means they are at the top of the food chain in their ecosystem, the ocean. Losing an apex predator species can cause devastating effects in an environment.

Today, roughly between one-fourth and one-third of shark species are vulnerable to extinction because of overfishing. What could happen if this continues and sharks disappear altogether?

If sharks
disappeared . . .

the ocean would no longer be balanced. Although different species have different diets, most sharks typically eat sick, slow, or weak prey, leaving the healthy animals to reproduce. If sharks disappeared . . .

the populations of seals, sea lions, and
other pinnipeds would potentially explode.

At higher populations,
they would eat more and
more fish, and eventually,

once there weren't any fish left,

they'd starve and die out, as well.

If fish and pinnipeds disappeared . . .

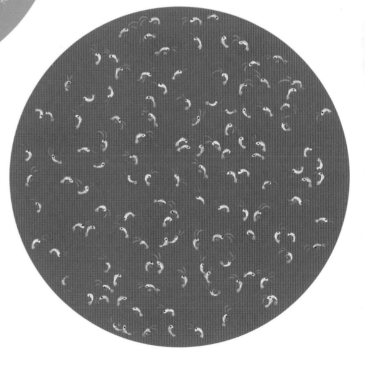

plankton, which is what many fish that are lower on the
food chain eat, could quickly grow out of control. That could
make the ocean a thick sludge. Nothing could survive in this
water. If the ocean became unlivable . . .

many species of land animals that rely on the ocean for food, such as seabirds and polar bears, could starve and die out.

The loss of those animals could cause still more
species farther inland to die out.

This pattern of cause and effect, called a trophic cascade, could spread
like a wave across countries and continents until animals around the
globe were affected, from bees, to birds, to bears, and eventually to . . .

US.

All species depend on one another to survive by keeping our planet's ecosystems in balance. And luckily, today . . . .

sharks still exist.

If we remember that we are all connected and if we work together, sharks—and our whole planet as we know it—will thrive. And maybe we'll see that what once seemed so scary . . .

isn't so scary after all.

GLOSSARY

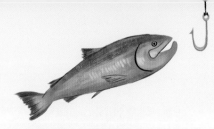

APEX PREDATOR: the top predator in an ecosystem.

BALANCE: when populations are at levels that allow all species to exist in harmony.

BIG BANG: the origin theory behind the universe. About 13.8 billion years ago, a single point expanded and created space, time, and matter.

BYCATCH: individuals from marine species that are accidentally trapped by fishing operations trying to catch a different species. Sharks are often caught unintentionally, and few are returned to the ocean alive or uninjured.

ECOSYSTEM: a system of living and nonliving things interacting in an environment.

ENVIRONMENT: all the living and nonliving things in a place or region.

EXTINCTION: the deaths, or inability to reproduce, of the last organisms of a species.

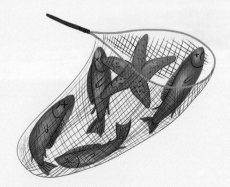

FOOD CHAIN: the network within which a living thing gets its food. In the ocean food chain, the "primary consumers" (small fish, crabs, jellyfish, shrimp) eat the "primary producers" (algae, krill). The "secondary consumers" (big fish, seals, otters, sea lions, dolphins, squids) eat the primary consumers. The "tertiary consumers" are the apex predators (sharks, killer whales, humans) that eat the secondary consumers.

NATURAL SELECTION: the very slow process by which a species adapts to its environment over many generations, making it easier for future generations to thrive. This occurs when individuals less suited to the environment die off, removing their genes from the gene pool.

OVERFISHING: taking more fish from a body of water than the remaining fish can replace by reproducing.

PINNIPED: various species of meat-eating four-limbed mammals that live in the water, such as seals and sea lions.

Rabbits 3-5 million years ago → Rabbits today!

PLANKTON: very small water-dwelling plants and animals that are primary producers in the ocean food chain.

SHARK FIN SOUP: a traditional Chinese or Vietnamese soup served on special occasions, such as at weddings.

Although the soup is considered a luxury item, it has become quite popular, and large numbers of sharks are killed just for their fins. Sometimes sharks are released alive after having their fins cut off, but they almost always die from blood loss or because they can't swim properly.

THRIVE: to grow well and succeed.

TROPHIC CASCADE: the chain of events that happens once a top predator is removed from or added to an ecosystem. These events can cause changes in the populations of all the other animals in the environment and dramatically shift the whole ecosystem, affecting other predators, prey, and nutrient levels.

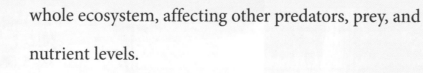